In this WMG Writer's Guide, *USA Today* bestselling author Dean Wesley Smith aims to shatter the myth that writing fast equals writing badly—or, conversely, writing well equals writing slowly—by showing how he wrote a novel (which was accepted and published with no rewrites by a traditional publisher) in just ten days.

The
WMG Writer's Guide
Series

HOW TO WRITE A NOVEL IN TEN DAYS

A WMG WRITER'S GUIDE

DEAN WESLEY SMITH

*wmg*PUBLISHING

How to Write a Novel in Ten Days

Copyright © 2014 by Dean Wesley Smith

All rights reserved

Published 2014 by WMG Publishing
www.wmgpublishing.com
Cover art © copyright Srapulsar38/Dreamstime
Book and cover design copyright © 2014 WMG Publishing
Cover design by Allyson Longueira/WMG Publishing
ISBN-13: 978-1-56146-603-0
ISBN-10: 1-56146-603-4

First published in slightly different form on Dean Wesley Smith's blog at www.deanwesleysmith.com in 2013.

Killing the Top Ten Sacred Cows of Publishing copyright © 2014 by Dean Wesley Smith

Contents

HOW TO WRITE A NOVEL IN TEN DAYS

A WMG WRITER'S GUIDE

INTRODUCTION

THIS BOOK is pretty easy to explain. It is simply a series of twelve blog posts, one per day, that I did over a stretch of 12 days just under a year ago. The point of the blogs was to detail out a novel I wrote for a traditional publisher in ten days. I had one post ahead of the writing days and one after I finished the book to wrap up.

All twelve are here.

Now granted, as each day went on, I added to the post, and at the end of the day I did a summary on each post. So if you were following this (as thousands were on my web site hour-by-hour), you would see each post grow as each day went on.

The goal of doing the blogs was to help take out the mystery of "writing" fast and show how it can be done easily. You just spend the time. Writing fast is not typing fast, it's just sitting in the chair and writing for numbers of hours.

A little background: I have written and sold over a hundred novels to traditional publishers over the last twenty-five years. Some years I wrote a great deal, some years I took off during

1

those twenty-five years and wrote no books. But after a hundred plus novels, I know how to write a novel.

I wrote this into the dark, as some writers call this type of writing. In other words, I had no outline. And the novel was published by the publisher with no rewrites from me.

I have left all the blog posts pretty much as I wrote them here in this book, because I felt that would be the best way to detail out the feeling of those ten days.

So I hope this journey through the daily writing process of a novel by a professional novelist is fun and entertaining and enlightening.

I had fun detailing out the process as well.

Enjoy the journey and have fun with your own writing.

—*Dean Wesley Smith*
February 10th, 2014
Lincoln City, Oregon

A BLOG POST ABOUT THE NOVEL...

AS I HAVE SAID a few times over the last six months, I was hired to write a ghost novel for a major author. I will never tell anyone who the author is or even why I am writing this for this author. Not a word. Ever, so don't ask. But I can tell you that when this comes out of New York, it will be a major bestseller because this author's books always are.

I have been paid the advance, so I plan on starting the novel next week as soon as this great workshop that is going on here at the coast is finished. Character Voice and Setting workshop. Wonderful fun. Great writers.

I will blog here about the writing process of the book, more than likely putting up five or six posts per day about each session and a post at the end of the day summing it all up.

I hope to write the book (70,000 words) in 7 to 10 days and then turn it in to the publisher. One draft.

So if you want to follow the writing process of a novel like this, learn how to write a novel in a short period of time, check back regularly.

I'll also tell you about the other things going on in my day as it goes along. And I will talk about my moods, my feelings, and so on about the writing.

I do not have an outline and will be just writing off into the dark on this one, so it might get kind of scary and entertaining. I hope, anyway, because I hate being bored when I write. (grin)

And I'll be glad to answer questions as it goes along about the writing process. (Not about the book itself in any fashion.)

See you soon. It will be fun for me. I hope it will entertain others in the actual writing process.

DAY ONE

AS I SAID in the previous post, I'm going to have posts here for the ghost novel writing process. (And no, this is not a novel about ghosts, this is me ghosting a novel because I was hired by a publisher.)

I will add to this post at different times today right up until I head to bed so you can follow the process. At the end of each post I will add up the daily word count and project word count. You want to see what a professional writer's day is like, I'll put it up here, every day until this book is done.

Here we go... this might be interesting in a perverse sort of way.

DAY 1, ENTRY 1:

12:45 PM: Rolled out of bed because my big, fluffy white cat—Walter White Kitty ... not my fault or his fault for that name...blame Kris (my wife, Kristine Kathryn Rusch)—decided I needed to be up and awake. (I went to bed about 5 am after watching far too much about the tragic events in Boston.)

1:15 PM: I got to my Internet computer with my breakfast bars and did e-mail and answered questions and such. It was luckily an easy morning.

1:45 PM: Moved to my writing computer, set up files, set up a chapter template since I keep a different file for every chapter and combine them at the end, then typed in a title, typed in the main character's name and started writing. I have no idea where this book is going, but to start I paid attention to making up some setting through the character's eyes and opinions.

2:20 PM: About 500 words done. Headed off to get the snail mail and then a meeting at WMG Publishing. At 3:15 met Kris for lunch since she had also been out and running around doing errands. Then back to WMG Publishing and then back here to my home office.

4:15 PM: checked my e-mail, had copyedits sent to me from an editor on a short story. He promised they were light, so I spent thirty minutes doing that and getting the story back to the editor. I then did other e-mail and workshop questions as well and did this first part of this post.

5:05 PM: headed back to my writing computer.

DAY 1, ENTRY 2:

5:05 PM: Moved over to my writing computer from my Internet computer and decided that before I went too far I needed to start a glossary of terms, character dress, place names and such, so I set that up and put in it the little bits I had done in the first 500 words.

Then wrote about 700 words until about 6 PM, took a five minute break, came back and wrote another 500 words before my cat, Walter (Or as Kris now calls him at times The Waltise Falcon) reminded me in no uncertain terms that it was time for a nap.

6:30 PM: checked my e-mail, answered one, grabbed the cat and headed for the downstairs media room to take a nap with the cat. Kris woke me at 7 and we watched news and ate dinner. I did the dishes, tossed in a load of laundry, and headed back for my office. I answered more e-mails, started one more thing for another editor that needs to be done this weekend, then wrote this second entry.

Time is now 8:15 PM and I am headed back to the writing computer. Total so far today around 1,700 words on the book. I'm feeling pretty good about the start so far.

DAY 1, ENTRY 3:

9:30 PM: (This is put up slightly late since the Internet connection was down until after four in the morning, but this is what I would have said.)

I did about 1,300 words between 8:15 and 9:45. Then a fire alarm here in the house went off without reason. Something silly like a dying battery. So by the time I fixed that, Kris offered me a snack so I had a snack with her, then headed back up to the WMG offices to work on some collectable books there as a break.

I got back around 11:00 and tried to put this entry up, but couldn't because of the Internet connection being down, so went to work. At that point I was at around 3,000 words and feeling really fine for the first day.

DAY 1, ENTRY 4:

From 11:00 PM until around midnight I did another session, another 800 words, then took a break and went downstairs to our media room and watched the news and part of Craig Ferguson with Kris.

12:45 AM: went back to work, did about another 1,000 words in just over an hour, took another break and again tried to get online. Kris was headed to bed, so she let me use her iPad to put up a comment to tell everyone what was happening, which was all it was allowing me to do.

2:00 AM: went back to the writing computer, got about another 1,000 words done in another hour. Took a short break, Internet connection still down. Went back to work.

3:00 AM: Internet connection still down, I did about another 1,000 words, but turned on my e-mail so that it would make a sound when an outgoing message finally got out.

4:10 AM: I did about another 1,000 words before my Internet computer dinged and told me the Internet was back up and working. So I stopped and came to this computer to do this post.

At this point at 4:26 in the morning, I'm at 7,625 words for the day. I could go a little farther but this is a ton better than I had hoped for the first day so I'm going to stop and go downstairs with my cat and veg out on some stupid television.

I still have no idea at all where this book is going. Just making it up as I go. But at the same time I'm feeling no worry at the moment either. I have a hunch that will come.

TOTAL:
Day #1—7,625 words

Feeling great, happy with the first day. Best first day on a novel I've had in some time, to be honest.

Back tomorrow for Day Two. (Remember, my day starts when I drag my butt out of bed, which considering I'll be watching television for the next hour to clear the damn book from my mind so I can sleep, getting out of bed will be around 1 PM.)

DAY TWO

AS I SAID in the previous post, I'm going to have one post per day here for the "ghost" novel writing process that I was hired by a New York publisher to do. I am aiming for 7 to 10 days to finish this novel. I can give ZERO hints about the content of the book, so please don't ask. I am only talking about the writing process and my day around the writing process.

I will add to this post at different times during the day right up until I head to bed so you can follow the process. At the end of each post I will add up the daily word count and project word count. You want to see what a professional writer's day is like, I'll put a post up here every day until this book is done.

Day One total word count was 7,625 words. So, now on to Day Two.

DAY 2, ENTRY 1:
1:15 PM: Rolled out of bed and by 1:45 PM I had my breakfast bars and was answering my e-mail and comments on Day 1

of this. Some good questions. Make sure if you are following this to read the comments and my answers on each day.

2:40 PM now... About one hour of email and comments. About normal for me. Now off to do the first session or two. Back later with another entry in this day.

DAY 2, ENTRY 2:

3:30 PM: I got about 700 words done in the first session, then Kris and I headed off to get the mail and have a quick lunch. Kris is in the last third of a new Kris Nelscott Smokey Dalton novel, so this house is great fun at the moment, since I'm living in this book and she's living in 1970 Chicago.

4:40 PM: Back from lunch and back to work. Got about 1,000 more words done before needing to take a break at 5:50 PM. The ocean outside my window is flat and it's a beautiful day here on the Oregon Coast. The sun is reflecting off the ocean and making this office heat up even though I have the window wide open, which the cats love. But that makes it hard to type at times, let me tell you. [I know, tiny violin. (grin)]

I answered some e-mail and then some comments. It's now 6:15 PM and I'm headed back to my writing computer for another session before naps with Walter White Kitty (Or as Kris is now calling him, the Waltese Falcon) before dinner.

Total original word count so far today 1,718 words.

DAY 2, ENTRY 3:

7:05 PM: I managed to get almost another thousand words from 6:15 PM. Then I took a break, grabbed the big fluffy white guy and headed for the basement for a nap. Kris woke me and the cat at 7:30 and we ate in front of the news. I did the dishes and headed back to my office.

8:30 PM: Answered e-mails and a number of questions in the comments. And wrote this far in this entry. It's now 8:55 and with a cup of tea in hand I'm headed back to my writing computer. Window over the ocean still open and the ocean air smells wonderful tonight.

Total so far today around 2,700 words.

DAY 2, ENTRY 4:

9:50 PM: I managed another 700 words. Slower than the other sessions because a new viewpoint character decided he/she needed to talk. Sigh. Had to create the character and that's just slower to start.

Then after 700 words I decided I needed a break and headed up to the WMG Publishing offices to work on sorting some collectables and organizing some stuff up there. I got back here about 10:50 and made myself another cup of tea and got a snack and am heading to the writing computer again.

So by 11:00 PM the day has managed around 3,400 words. About on pace. I'm feeling fine as well, not in the slightest bit tired. So far this has not been a strain in the slightest. Tomorrow may be another matter.

DAY 2, ENTRY 5:

12:10 AM: I managed yet another thousand words or so from 11:00 PM. Ran right into a tough scene, stopped cold. So I went downstairs and watched a show with Kris in the media room. Now I feel like going at it again.

It's 1:20 AM and I'm headed back to the writing computer. Back later for one final Day 2 update and the totals so far at that point.

DAY 2, ENTRY 6:

2:10 AM: I finished another 1,000 or so words from 1:20 until 2:10, then took a break. Got back to the writing computer at 2:30 AM.

3:50 AM. I wrote pretty much straight through from 2:30 with only a minor break to move around. Then I flat ran out of gas. Brain said, "Go to bed." But I didn't type that. (grin)

Me and the white cat are headed downstairs to veg on television for a short time before heading to bed.

My daily word count is 7,734 words for Day Two.

TOTALS:
Day #1—7,625 words
Day #2—7,734 words
Total so far—15,359 words.

On pace and on target, which surprises me, to be honest. I am always slower up front, so if I follow pattern I will pick up more words by Thursday or Friday and maybe even finish it Friday or Saturday. We shall see. Lots of slips between here and there. (grin)

See you all for Day Three.

DAY THREE

DAY 3, ENTRY 1:

12:45 PM: Rolled out of bed and by 1:15 PM I had my breakfast bars and was answering my e-mail and comments on Day 2 of this. Some good questions. Make sure if you are following this to read the comments and my answers on each day.

I finished most of the questions and my e-mail just before 2:00 PM and then Kris and I headed off to the normal Sunday writer lunch. Eight other professional fiction writers there today besides us. Great conversation.

Got back here around 4:00 PM, answered more questions and some more e-mail and did this post, and am now, at 4:20 PM heading over to my writing computer for my first session.

DAY 3, ENTRY 2:

4:20 PM: I worked for about an hour, took a five minute break. Ended up with pretty close to 1,000 words in that hour. That seems to be about the pace this book is flowing at. I sometimes only go around 800 words per hour with my four-finger typing, but this one, in most places, is flowing nicely.

5:30 PM: went back for a second session and finished another thousand words. It's now 6:32 and I'm headed to the media room to take a nap with good old Walter White Kitty. (And yes, at some point I'll put a picture of the guy here during this week.)

Total so far on Day 3... Around 2,000 words.

DAY 3, ENTRY 3:

Walter and I napped until 7:00 PM. Then we had dinner and I got back to my office around 7:30 PM. ·

10:00 PM: I haven't done another word on the novel yet tonight. From 7:30 until about ten minutes ago I was working on the Cliffhangers workshop. For those of you who don't know, I teach some online workshops and each of the writers in the online workshop turn in an assignment each week if they want. So I write them each a letter talking about their assignment, then do a video that talks about the assignment in general and I put it up with the following week's videos.

If you want any information about the online workshops, the descriptions and how to sign up are up under the Online Workshops tab.

10:10 PM: headed back to my writing computer finally. I still have some workshop stuff to do later in the evening, but I can do that on breaks.

DAY 3, ENTRY 4:

10:10 PM: I headed back to my writing computer and managed to get about 1,000 more words done by 11:00 PM.

I took a break, read the March 15th issue of *Publisher's Weekly*, had a snack, and went back to work at about 11:15 PM:

I managed yet another 1,000 words and then came to do this entry. Right now it's just after midnight and I'm going to go get a snack and get back to it.

Total so far today around 4,000 words.

DAY 3, ENTRY 5:

1:00 AM: I made it back to the writing computer just after midnight and in fifty minutes managed about another 1,000 words. That sure seems to be my output for a session on this book. That's great. I always like books that do this, much more than the books that won't let me do more than 800 words a session.

Then I took a break and worked on some more workshop stuff, this one for a coast workshop. The difference between the coast workshops here we do five or so times per year and the online workshops is that the coast workshops are like graduate level workshops, while the online workshops are for all levels. The coast workshops are invite only as well. Then went back to the computer and got another few hundred words done before hitting a point I felt stuck.

1:30 AM: So now to a break and then back to write the next sentence. I don't think this is a major stuck, more of a type of stuck that I just got ahead of the back of my brain is all. Ten minutes and I'll be back at it.

Still not a clue at all where this book is going. Not one. But I am liking the characters I came up with, so that's helping. Now if I just don't have to kill one of them along the way. (grin)

DAY 3, ENTRY 6:

1:45 AM: Fired on, clearly not stuck at all like I thought. I just needed a break so my fingers stopped and pretended I was stuck. They do that when I try to continue on too long in one session. (grin)

I got another 1,000 or so words done by 2:30 AM before taking a short break and working on the workshop stuff I had to do.

2:45 AM: back at the fiction computer, got another 1,000 or so words done. It's now 3:40 and I'm out of steam. I have done more work on the workshop as well and might spend a few more minutes on that before heading to bed.

TOTALS:
Day #1—7,625 words
Day #2—7,734 words
Day #3—7,059 words
Total so far—22,418 words

This still feels like a 7 or 8 day pace. We shall see how the next few days go and if it picks up speed some. If not, I'm looking at 9 days. But I'm pretty happy with this start so far.

DAY FOUR

DAY 4, ENTRY 1:

12:45 PM: Rolled out of bed this morning at the same time as yesterday, even though I had ended up watching a stand-up comic last night until 5:30 in the morning. Ah, well. By 1:15 PM I had my breakfast bars and was answering my e-mail and comments on Day 3 of this. Some good questions. Make sure if you are following this to read the comments and my answers on each day.

2:15 PM: I finished the comments and questions and basic e-mail. And finished getting up the online workshop response for the Cliff-hangers Workshop I should have finished last night but spaced it. Now I'm heading out to get the mail and head up to WMG Publishing to see what's happening up there. (I'll cause my normal hour of disruption at WMG and then head back here, grabbing some lunch on the way.)

DAY 4, ENTRY 2:

5:00 PM: Not one new fiction word yet written, but headed to the writing computer shortly. I spent time at the post office, then one bank, then up to WMG where I helped them deal with setting up a web site that will hold a novel of Kris's that WMG is going to be serializing starting tomorrow. Check out www.WMGPublishing.com for that. It's a brand new novel called *Spree*. A wonderful mystery.

Then I went to yet another bank, then grabbed some lunch at Subway and came home and ate it with Kris while she ate her lunch as well. Then back to this computer to answer more e-mails and do more workshop stuff, and now doing this entry. So now, just a minute or so before 5 PM I'm headed for my writing computer for the first time today.

It's a beautiful day on the Oregon Coast, but the ocean outside my window is a little rough from a north wind. And it's scary bright in here, especially for a person used to working at night. (grin)

DAY 4, ENTRY 3:

7:00 PM: Over the last two hours I answered more e-mail and comments on a break between writing sessions and managed 1,800 words as well in two different writing sessions.

So now, as is normal for me, Walter White Kitty and I are headed for the dark media room downstairs to take a short nap before dinner.

So 1,800 words so far total today.

DAY 4, ENTRY 4:

9:30 PM: Nap and dinner were done around 8:15 and then I answered a few questions and e-mails, did a little work on a workshop, and went back to the writing computer for another session. I managed another 1,000 words or so in an hour.

Now I'm taking a break, going to work on the Pitches and Blurbs workshop with the writers taking that online class, and then go back to writing. That's the plan, anyway. Just under 3,000 words so far today total. About right, especially for a Monday that had a lot of other things going on.

DAY 4, ENTRY 5:

11:30 PM: I spent most of the last two hours working on the Online Workshop Pitches and Blurbs, getting the assignments back to the writers and doing a video response. Then I wrote a quick 500 words and am now heading for the media room to watch The Voice, the best show ever done to show how artists at top levels work and are trained. It's a stunner and a must-see for anyone wanting to be a writer. So much knowledge.

Back after a time.

DAY 4, ENTRY 6:

2:30 AM: I watched all two hours of The Voice. Stunning stuff about art and being an artist. Then I came back up to this computer, did a little more workshop stuff, then went and wrote.

In two sessions with a short break I did around 1,500 more words. So by my rough count I'm in about 5,000 words so far today. I'll add it all up later when I finish tonight. Still got some energy left, surprising on a day like today and all the errands and work and workshop stuff.

DAY 4, ENTRY 7:

4:00 AM: Brain just never got back on it tonight. Too much stuff, too many distractions today, which I had fully expected for a Monday. So I'm heading to the big screen to veg over some bad television and then to bed.

Today I also made it through that deadly one-third spot in any novel (1/3 of 70,000 words is 23,300 words) where the energy is gone, everything seems like a pile a crap, and you lose interest in the book and even writing more. I have never had a novel that I didn't go through that. It's where most beginning novelists stop cold. Professional novelists know about this and just power through.

I went through it today, actually this afternoon. So that feels good as well to have that barrier behind me.

Even though this was a lower word count day, I still feel great about the entire process and feel like I am right on target for an eight or nine day novel without problems. I always have lower word count days, usually the first and fourth days. The next tough day will be Thursday, but I might be on a roll by then, so I'm not going to worry about it now.

Barring unforseens, tomorrow might be my first 10,000 word day. We shall see.

TOTALS:
Day #1—7,625 words
Day #2—7,734 words
Day #3—7,059 words
Day #4—5,070 words
Total so far—27,488 words

DAY FIVE

DAY 5, ENTRY 1:
2:50 PM: Rolled out of bed at 1:20 PM and made it to my computer with my breakfast bars by 1:50 PM. Since then I've been answering comments and e-mails. Folks, the most important part of this is the comments after each day and during the day. I do my best to answer each question honestly. So make sure to read them all. It will be worth your time. You might discover a myth you didn't even know you were holding.

Now off to my writing computer.

Back later...

DAY 5, ENTRY 2:
6:50 PM: I managed a session of about 900 words, took a break, had a quick lunch that Kris brought back after she had run the errands today. Then I went back and got another 900 words done before Kris and I took off for the grocery store.

I stopped at Goodwill for a few minutes, found nothing, then we went to the store. A bunch of locals were there and we ended up talking for a time, got back around 6:00PM.

At 6:00 PM I sat down for a third afternoon session and got another 900 or so words. Now it's 6:50 PM and I'm headed for the regular nap with my white cat downstairs.

Total so far today about 2,800 words.

DAY 5, ENTRY 3:

10:00 PM: Nap and dinner and news. I think I made it back up here around 8:00 PM. Last two hours I was working on the homework for the essentials workshop and doing the taping of my response to this week's assignment. This was a fun assignment and it was fun to read what the eleven writers in the Essentials workshop turned in this last week.

(I'll do a post about the workshops starting the first week of May and the ones starting the first week of June... still openings in all of them. Under the Online Workshop tab at the top of the page.)

So now it's about 10:00 PM and I'm heading back to my writing computer. Another update after a time...

DAY 5, ENTRY 4:

12:47 AM: I wrote for two sessions, both fairly short from 10:00 until around 11:30 and ended up getting closer to 4,000 words for the day.

At 11:30 PM I went down to the media room to watch The Voice. Then watched a great interview with Carol Burnett and the star of Arrow on The Tonight Show. Now back up here, answering questions and heading back to my writing computer.

It's now 12:51 AM. Need a new cup of tea and then I'm off to writing. We shall see how it goes from here for the rest of the evening...

DAY 5, ENTRY 5:

4:30 AM: I was typing along and I felt I was about halfway done with this book, so I stopped and decided to add it all up. And behold, I am. Good place to stop for the night.

I did three of sessions since 1:00 AM, and did some workshop stuff as well. Each session turned out to be around a thousand words or so. That seems to be normal for me, hitting a stride after midnight or one for a few hours.

So at this point the pace is still nine days for me unless I don't pick up speed or get stuck or have a bad day. If that happens, this will take ten days. (I do plan on picking up speed for the next four days, but we shall see. Some books just don't allow that to happen. But I would love to be done late Saturday night instead of Sunday night. No reason other than I want to finish putting together *Fiction River* Volume Three: *Time Streams* that I am editing and I have other stories to write.)

TOTALS:
Day #1—7,625 words
Day #2—7,734 words
Day #3—7,059 words
Day #4—5,070 words
Day #5—7,786 words
Total so far—35,274 words.

DAY SIX

I'M ABOUT HALFWAY to my hoped-for-and-contracted-word-count of 70,000 words. Seemingly right on schedule for my ten day pace. So we shall see how the next half of this goes.

As far as the plot, I still have NO IDEA at all where this is heading. But I am having fun writing it. I know that bothers many people who fear writing into the dark, but at the moment it's great fun for me. The characters are just moving forward and occasionally I get to the end of a chapter or scene and know what needs to be in the next chapter. But that's it. I hope in a few days to have some idea how this will end. I'll let you know when that happens.

Or if I get stuck.

Now off into the second half of the novel and Day 6.

DAY 6, ENTRY 1:

3:30 PM: Rolled out of bed at 1:30 today and got to the Internet computer around 2:15 with my breakfast bars. It's a stunningly beautiful day here today, with the ocean a little rough from a light wind. Last night as I was writing I was sneezing like crazy, driving poor old Walter White Kitty nuts. I'd sneeze and he'd yell at me. Not sure what he was saying, but I know where the sneezing was coming from. I had my office window open and the wind was out of the east, something it rarely is here, so all the crap from the Portland valley was blowing over this way. I must be allergic to something growing over there. Thankfully, today the wind is shifting back off the ocean so there is clean air again like we are used to here.

I had a ton of e-mail and workshop stuff to answer this morning, so it's now 3:30 PM and I'm headed to the writing computer for a session before heading out to WMG Publishing offices and the snail mail.

Later...

DAY 6, ENTRY 2:

4:15 PM: I wrote about 500 words, then realized I was running late and jumped out of here to head for the post office. I then stopped by WMG Publishing and went down and talked to the fine folks at Ella Distribution for a few short minutes, then grabbed some Burger King and came home.

5:00 PM: While eating I heard a noise outside and opened the door to find a long-haired gray cat spooked off the porch and under the car. So I got him/her some food and it came right back up to eat. Clearly hungry. We thought it a neighbor's cat the first few times we saw it, but now we're not so sure anymore. It is thin and too hungry to be a neighbor's cat. We just hadn't seen it much. So now it looks like I'll be trapping and taking in another cat. Sigh...

5:45 PM: Finally got back to the writing computer after answering a few more e-mails. I got another 1,100 words in. It's now 6:45 and I'm going to head back to another thirty minute writing session before heading down to the media room for a nap with the Waltese Falcon, as Kris calls him.

DAY 6, ENTRY 3:

8:00 PM: I got back up here and started into the homework on the Ideas workshop, working my way slowly through that and then recording the response video for the week. I was finished with that about 10:00. Some great stuff in those assignments, fun reading.

10:00 PM: Finished the workshop homework for the night, answered a few e-mail, and then Kris came in and told me her new blog was done, so I went out to the kitchen and read that. It's a great one, about taking chances. She's talking this week about something we do so normally around here it's like breathing, but most writers don't. In fact, the myths I've been pounding at here in all these comments are about writers afraid to try something new or something they believe "won't work for me." Anyway, it's a great column and it will be up tomorrow morning like normal (Thursday) on her site, so read it, folks.

10:30 PM: headed back to my writing computer as soon as I get a cup of tea. Not sure how far in I am today. I think I'm past a couple thousand words, not great, but considering the day, not bad. I'll add it up later.

DAY 6, ENTRY 4:

11:45 PM: Taking a short break. Back later with a writing update…

DAY 6, ENTRY 5:

1:45 AM: Not a clue how much I have done, but it doesn't feel like enough. For some reason really tired tonight. I haven't lost the will to live yet, but there is no doubt I am dragging on this book at the moment.

Might have something to do with the fact that I still don't have a clue where this thing is going. Or that I ended up doing far too many other things today, including just spending an hour plus watching television instead of writing.

So now I'm going to go back to my writing computer and do what I tell other writers to do: Write the next line.

I'll be back later with the end of the day numbers and such.

DAY 6, ENTRY 6:

4:15 AM: I'm giving up, even though I have a hunch I could go farther tonight and do another session, another 800 words. I just flat don't feel like it, so headed for the basement to watch some really bad television, then go to bed.

Somehow in the last few hours I managed to write another 2,500 words or so, so the day ended up better than I had expected when I added it all up. I had over 2,000 words done before I went for a nap, dinner, and then did the homework for the online workshop. And it seems I did another 2,500 or so words before going down to watch some television earlier.

Then I managed another 2,500 or so in the last few sessions, with five minute breaks and doing about 800 or so words per session. So maybe this is picking up speed a little.

If I can get a fairly clear day on Thursday, Friday, and Saturday, I still might finish this in nine days. Again, we shall see because I still don't know where it's going. But I am getting there at a decent and pretty consistent clip. (grin)

TOTALS:

Day #1—7,625 words

Day #2—7,734 words

Day #3—7,059 words

Day #4—5,070 words

Day #5—7,786 words

Day #6—7,116 words

Total so far—42,380 words.

And that, folks, is how you write a short novel in 6 days.

You ever wonder how writers like Lester Dent (Doc Savage), Max Brand, and other pulp writers and mystery writers in the fifties and sixties did it, that was how. Take one day off and start again. Four short novels a month. And I taught workshops and did a bunch of other stuff at the same time.

And got full night's sleep every night.

Now onward to a novel of 70,000 words because that what this stupid contract says and I still don't have a climax, let alone an ending. But I will. I will.

I trust the process.

DAY SEVEN

DAY 7, ENTRY 1:

2:30 PM: Rolled out of bed by 1:15 PM today and was in here with my breakfast bars by 1:45. Now done with e-mail and comments, so headed to the writing computer before Kris comes get me to head out for errands and lunch and shopping and such.

Back with a word count later...

DAY 7, ENTRY 2:

10:30 PM: Wow, does this day suck so far. Yes, that time is 10:30 PM: late in the evening... I have about 1,200 words done so far and haven't done the homework yet for the workshop. So off to do that next, then back to the book.

Just too much business stuff today. Sigh... Kris and I went out for errands, had lunch, I wrote a little, she wrote a little, and then business all evening. Now back in my office. And somehow I need to get my mind back on this book. (grin)

DAY 7, ENTRY 3:

2:30 AM: Well, this day is a great example of life getting in the way. After that last entry even more business came up and had to be worked through and talked about. But I did get the homework done for the workshop and all that.

I think I have around 1,500 words done so far today, but going to get back at this now and see what I can manage. I fully expected to do upwards of 10,000 words today... yeah... so much for expectations... (grin) Just far, far too much business stuff I'm afraid.

So, not only is this an example of how to write regularly, it's an example of how to work through life being tossed at you.

Now over to the writing computer and see if I can remember where I was before all this crap hit the fan...

DAY 7, ENTRY 4:

4:00 AM: Two fairly intense sessions of about 700 words each session, both lasting about forty minutes, and I'm burnt to a crisp after today.

I'm going to go watch some bad television and then go to bed.

TOTALS:
Day #1—7,625 words
Day #2—7,734 words
Day #3—7,059 words
Day #4—5,070 words
Day #5—7,786 words
Day #6—7,116 words
Day #7—3,005 words
Total so far—45,385 words.
(Just over 24,000 words to go...)

I'm stunned I even managed those two sessions today to be honest. With luck, tomorrow will be a better day and I'll be back on track. Stay tuned.

I promised you I would be honest with the word count and the days and what happens to a point. It suppose it was too much to ask from life for me to get an open nine or ten days of writing without business crashing in and throwing around a few fun things to deal with. But they are dealt with for the moment, now back to writing for the weekend.

Still aiming for Sunday and ten days on this.

DAY EIGHT

DAY 8, ENTRY 1:

5:30 PM: Rolled out of bed by 1:30 PM today and was in here with my breakfast bars by 2:00 PM. I managed to get some of my e-mail and stuff done here, but then got called away into business meetings with a business lawyer and then I had lunch with Kris and stopped up at WMG for a time.

Now back here.

I'm going to do a little more e-mail and such and then shift over to the writing chair and get going on the book, work to have a good day if not a great day on it. Yeah, I know, starting late today, but it's Friday night and I'm old and got nothing better to do but write.

DAY 8, ENTRY 2:

7:15 PM: Well, I'm back on a roll again. In two sessions with only a few minute break between them, I managed almost 2,500 words in just under two hours. Now that's rocket speed for me. (Pent up typing I guess.)

And in the middle of it my subconscious tossed in a nasty plot twist that will take some pages to resolve, but I guess my subconscious was telling me I didn't have enough book.

Who knows. I just trust the process and try to stay out of the way.

I'm sure all of you out there are having a good Friday night. Watching a person like me write would be like watching paint dry. Only way watching paint dry would be fun would be with a lot of booze, some loud music, and lots of great friends. And the wet paint would have to be on someone you find attractive. (grin)

But I'm here alone, I don't drink anymore, and my oldies station is turned down low. Kris is buried in writing the new Smokey Dalton novel, so she's living in 1970. So I think I'll live for a time longer in the book I'm writing.

That said, however, the sun is streaming in over the Pacific right now, making this office far too bright for a night person like me. So I'm grabbing the cat and heading for a nap.

Back later...

DAY 8, ENTRY 3:

9:30 PM: Fed, nap, and watched the news. Ready to fire again. Now just have to shift Walter White Kitty from napping on my writing chair to napping on this Internet chair and I can get writing again.

No writing workshop homework tonight, so just straight back to writing...

DAY 8, ENTRY 4:

11:30 PM: Two sessions since 9:30 with a quick run to the store between them. I managed another 2,000 words bringing the total to pretty close to 4,500 so far today.

Interesting as I was headed to the grocery store around 10:15, it felt like when I would head out to the casino about that time of night on a Friday night. Over the years that was my favorite time to play poker since the rookies were drinking and getting tired and were tossing money around like it was something they didn't care about. I would come in, join the table, and take their money for a few hours and be home by three in the morning.

Felt weird going out like that again and not going to the casino.

On the book side of things, I finally figured out the ending and climax. Yeah!! About 18,000 to 20,000 words left to write, so pretty much on target and I think the climax of the book and the ending will take in that word range to write.

I actually was starting to get a little worried earlier as my subconscious snuck in a nifty plot twist which felt like it would take a lot of words to write. The very LAST thing I want is a work-for-hire novel being one word longer than what they are paying me for.

So now off to a break to watch a little television, then back for more words. I will report in a couple more times tonight.

DAY 8, ENTRY 5:

2:30 AM: Give or take... watched too much television tonight. Not sure why, just felt like it on a Friday night. More than likely because I figured out the ending and now I'm bored. Sigh...

I'm still just under 5,000 words for the day. Better get going so I can finish this thing on Sunday. Get it turned in on Monday.

DAY 8, ENTRY 6:

5:30 AM: Give or take... got tired an hour or so back and gave up and went back to watch bad television. So didn't turn out to be a great day, just an okay day.

TOTALS:
Day #1—7,625 words
Day #2—7,734 words
Day #3—7,059 words
Day #4—5,070 words
Day #5—7,786 words
Day #6—7,116 words
Day #7—3,005 words
Day #8—7,473 words
Total so far—52,858 words

Just over 17,000 words to go... and I know where I am going now and am bored... sigh... I hate knowing the ending of something I am writing...

DAY NINE

DAY 9, ENTRY 1:
   4:45 PM: Horrid slow start on this fine Saturday. Managed to get out of bed later than normal and have been doing e-mail and working on business stuff with Kris. Of course this turned out to be a week of major business things. Figures....
   I should be at this after I head out for a quick lunch, then back here for some writing.

DAY 9, ENTRY 2:
   7:30 PM: I went out to the auction and had a great time working with the owner there over some collectables, then grabbed myself some lunch and the mail, then got back here and did two quick sessions. So far around 1,800 words total for the day.
   Now off to nap with the cat.

DAY 9, ENTRY 3:

11:00 PM: The ending on this caused me to make a major change in the plot, so I went back to the beginning and changed that detail and wrote some new scenes and such around that one major detail shift. Then ran forward, so about 2,000 new words since about 9 PM, plus the changes.

No, that was not rewriting, that was a detail shift that was required by something I found two hundred pages later, that required new words inserted in a few places up in the front of the book. That is what I call "cycling" or "fixing."

If I wrote like Kris writes, she would have made a note and kept typing forward and then gone back on a "fix" draft and put that in. But since I am mailing this book tomorrow night to the editor, I needed to fix it now, the moment I realized the needed detail insertion.

Note: the reader getting to the end will think the author was brilliant because he could plant such information and have it turn up later in the book. Or they will think the author must have really outlined the book to make sure such information was up front that was needed later.

I am not brilliant nor did I outline. I'm just not afraid of going back and adding in a detail. No big deal.

Powering forward...

DAY 9, ENTRY 4:

1:45 AM: I did another thousand words, then went up to WMG Offices and dinged around up there for a time because I just felt like I needed to for no reason at all that I could think of. Then came back, watched an hour of news and television, now back up here in my office for the rest of the evening.

Seems this book is just not speeding up or slowing down. Just normal days dinging along on this.

I'm around 5,000 words so far today, so we shall see how this ends up.

DAY 9, ENTRY 5:

3:30 AM: I did another couple thousand words in just under two hours, with one short break to get something to drink.

Still going...night not finished yet.

DAY 9, ENTRY 6:

6:30 AM: I'm up a little late tonight. Wrote until after 5, then went and watched some bad television.

Managed about 2,500 more words. Total for the day is 9,373 words.

TOTALS:

Day #1—7,625 words
Day #2—7,734 words
Day #3—7,059 words
Day #4... 5,070 words
Day #5—7,786 words
Day #6—7,116 words
Day #7—3,005 words
Day #8—7,473 words
Day #9—9,373 words
Total so far—62,231 words.

Within sight...

DAY TEN

DAY 10, ENTRY 1:

4:45 PM: Normal Sunday start today. Got up around 1:00 PM, managed some e-mail before heading off to the professional writer's lunch at 2:00 PM. Got back around 3:45 PM and am now done with e-mail and comments for the moment.

So headed toward my writing computer to get a session done. Later tonight I need to do a few hours on the online workshop that I am teaching called Cliffhangers. I need to get letters about assignments back to everyone and my in general response recorded.

But even with that and the lunch today, I don't see much worry about finishing tonight. I seem to be powering right along just fine and dandy. Ending is in sight and it seems to be coming in close enough to the 70,000 word number to make my editor happy in New York.

We shall see when the day is over what the actual number will be.

I want to thank you all as well for the great comments and questions. If you haven't read all the questions and comments on every day, you want to make sure you do that. You never know what tiny bit of information from somewhere will help you with your own writing.

Now off to write and finish this novel so I can get started on something of my own again, plus I have at least three short stories editors are waiting for.

DAY 10, ENTRY 2:

6:45 PM: Managed just over 2,000 words in the last two hours. Firing right along now toward the ending...

Now off to the standard nap. White cat is waiting for me at the top of the stairs pretending to be asleep.

DAY 10, ENTRY 3:

10:00 PM: I had a nap and dinner and then came back here to my office and worked on the homework assignments for the Cliffhanger workshop, then did the video here in my office as well for that workshop. Too lazy at the moment to go up to the WMG Publishing offices where I normally record the videos.

So now, with the homework done, e-mails mostly answered, I'm headed back to my writing computer. Make a run at the end of this thing so I can get all my chapter files combined into one file and the entire novel sent off to the New York editor. And then they will owe me money again, which, of course, knowing traditional publishers as well as I do, won't arrive until August and then only after I scream for a time.

Ahh, I hate that part of this business.

Back to the fun part, the writing.

DAY 10, ENTRY 4:
11:00 PM: Taking a break...powered out about 1,200 words in an hour before needing to stop for five minutes. This much faster pace is normal for me near the end of a book. Not sure if I write more because I want the stupid thing over, or I write more because I'm bored and need to go fast to get finished.

3,200 approximately done for the day so far, plus lunch with writers and all the homework done for the workshop I'm teaching.

On schedule...

Not a clue how much more.

Back to typing...

DAY 10, ENTRY 5:
12:15 AM: another 1,000 words done before another break.

DAY 10, ENTRY 6:
2:30 AM: Done.

TOTALS:
Day #1—7,625 words
Day #2—7,734 words
Day #3—7,059 words
Day #4—5,070 words
Day #5—7,786 words
Day #6—7,116 words
Day #7—3,005 words
Day #8—7,473 words
Day #9 –9,373 words
Day #10—6,719 words
Total—68,950 words

I still have to spend fifteen minutes and combine it into one file and fire it off to the editor. But the writing is done.

The ending worked out fine and came quickly, as I expected. I'm slightly under the 70,000 words asked for in the contract, but not enough to worry about.

Ten days, pretty normal days for me, actually. I taught the online workshops, did a ton of business, read, watched television, and mostly got full nights sleep each night.

In other words, I did nothing different this week except do more blog posts than I normally would do and answer more comments than I normally answer in a week. But that was fun as well.

Remember, the total is only original fiction words in the last ten days. It does not count hundreds of e-mails, all the workshop letters in the workshops I am teaching, or all the comments answered in these posts. I don't count any of that, or these blogs either which were just over 1,000 words each for ten days.

The only thing important to a fiction writer like me is new fiction words.

I hope this exercise was worth the time for those of you watching. It wasn't much unusual for me except that this novel contract allowed me to do this.

Good luck everyone fighting the myths that stop you.

Writing really is fun. If you let it be fun.

THE DAY AFTER

I JUST FINISHED close to a 70,000 words on a novel I was hired to do by a New York publisher. Did it in ten days here and blogged about my days and how I did the words. The editor on the book reported that it arrived just fine.

Someone local came up to me today and congratulated me on finishing the book and I said, "Congratulations on going to work today." I do not think the person understood.

Numbers of people seemed stunned that I could go to work for ten days, then go to work on day #11. So for one more day, I'll do my day here. Just to try to put one more nail in the attempt at killing a few ugly myths about how writers work.

Now for one more day of watching paint dry.

THE DAY AFTER, ENTRY 1:

8:30 PM: Horrid start to the day, but alas I'm back here. A couple of the days in the novel writing I didn't get into the office until late to write, so back at this like normal.

The day started early for me as well, getting up around 12:00, getting my three breakfast bars eaten while doing some e-mail and then heading to the WMG offices by 1:30 PM. Meetings on all sorts of business stuff, then Kris and I had lunch and I went back for more meeting from 4 until 6:00 PM.

Then I went down to a local restaurant to enjoy part of a birthday celebration for a friend, then to the grocery store and back home to cook Kris dinner. We watched the news, I came up here to my office, worked on e-mail and did this. I will now work on the homework for the online workshop I am teaching called Pitches and Blurbs, then head back to the WMG Offices for a time.

I expect to be back here in my office at home by around 11:00 PM and headed for the writing computer. Up at WMG Publishing tonight I'll work on putting together *Fiction River: Time Streams* that I am editing so I can get that turned in on time. When I get back here I'll tell you what I end up writing on and give page counts.

THE DAY AFTER, ENTRY 2:

10:35 PM: Back from the WMG Publishing offices. Got my response recorded up there tonight for the workshop and got it loaded to the workshop site, then ended up spending thirty minutes talking with the landlord, who has a shop in the back of the building and is never there at night. He's a great guy.

So didn't work on the *Fiction River* editing, but instead came back here, did some more workshop work, now headed for my writing computer. At some point I'll go downstairs to watch The Voice. (As I have said before, a writer can learn a ton from this show if you understand what you are watching.)

THE DAY AFTER, ENTRY 3:

2:15 AM: I worked for about 45 minutes at a new Jukebox short story for *Time Streams* anthology, got about 600 words in, took a break and a short nap on the couch outside my office. Kris woke me up twenty minutes later and we went and watched The Voice and Castle.

Now I'm back in my office and headed back to the short story. Again, a slow start today because of all the business stuff, but still pretty normal. Tomorrow will be back to normal because I have ZERO meetings scheduled. (grin)

THE DAY AFTER, ENTRY 4 (THE LAST):

3:00 AM: I finally decided I'm done with this experiment to blog about my writing of a ghost novel. So this is the last entry, even though I will be up for a time longer writing.

I finished another 700 words or so on the time travel story. Title at the moment is "Home is a Song." That might change, but so far it is fitting. I'll keep going and get it done tonight or tomorrow, but not going to post the words or anything here.

I also have a thriller I wrote that I need to dig out of my files and get turned into WMG Publishing by Wednesday so it can get into the proof and production stages, so going to do that tomorrow. (Not rewrite, just dig it out and turn it in. A book called "Dead Money" already written, never sold.)

I have a new blog post coming on things in indie publishing on Thursday or Friday in my New World of Publishing series. I've been working on that in spare moments and I think it might be something a lot of writers have not thought about, but since it wasn't fiction, I didn't count it any more than I counted these.

So that's it. After 11 days of this silliness, back to regularly scheduled posts... I have writing to do...

BONUS CONTENT!

IF YOU LIKED *How to Write a Novel in Ten Days,* you might also like Dean Wesley Smith's *Killing the Top Ten Sacred Cows of Publishing.* Following is the second chapter of that book. The full book is available in ebook and trade paperback from your favorite bookseller.

Sacred Cow #2

WRITING FAST IS BAD

O r said in myth fashion: **WRITING SLOW EQUALS WRITING WELL**. Or the flip side: **WRITING FAST EQUALS WRITING POORLY**.

This comes out of everyone's mouth at one point or another in a form of apology for our work. "Oh, I just cranked that off."

Or the flip side… "This is some of my best work. I've been writing it for over a year."

Now this silly idea that the writing process has anything at all to do with quality of the work has been around in publishing for just over 100 years now, pushed mostly by the literature side and the college professors.

It has no basis in any real fact when it comes to writers. **None.** If you don't believe me, start researching how fast some of the classics of literature were written.

But don't ask major professional writers out in public. Remember we know this myth and lie about how really hard we do work. (Yup, that's right, someone who makes stuff up for a living will lie to you. Go figure.) So you have to get a long-term professional writer in a private setting. Then maybe with a few drinks under his belt the pro will tell you the truth about any project.

In my Writing in Public posts this year, I am doing my best to knock some of this myth down and just show what a normal day in a life can produce, even with me doing a bunch of other things at the same time.

My position:

NO WRITER IS THE SAME. NO PROJECT IS THE SAME.

And put simply:

THE QUALITY OF THE FINAL PRODUCT HAS NO RELATIONSHIP TO THE SPEED, METHOD, OR FEELING OF THE WRITER WHILE WRITING.

That's right, one day I could write some pages feeling sick, almost too tired to care, where every word is a pain, and the next day I write a few more pages feeling good and the words flowing freely and a week later I won't be able to tell which day was which from the writing.

How I feel when I write makes no difference to the quality of what I produce. None. Damn it, it should, but it just doesn't.

And I just laugh when a myth like this one attempts to lump all writers into the same boat and make us all write exactly the same way book after book after book.

No writer works the same, even from book to book or short story to short story.

In fact, as you will discover watching me over this year of writing in public, I don't do any story or novel similar to any other.

Talk to any writer, and I mean privately, and you will discover that one of the writer's books was written quickly, maybe even in a few weeks, while another book took the writer a half year to finish and he was deathly ill during half the writing time. And you, as a reader, reading the two books, would never be able to tell the difference.

But yet, traditional publishing, college professors, and just about anyone who even thinks about the writer behind the words has a belief system that words must be struggled over to be good.

Well, yes, sometimes.

And sometimes not.

Sometimes a writer gets into a white-hot heat and a book flows faster than the writer can type, getting done in just a number of days or weeks. And sometimes it just doesn't work that way.

Sometimes a writer has a deadline to hit and pushes to hit it, spending more hours in the chair, thus calling it writing fast. Some writers think and research a book for a few months, then write it in a few weeks. Some writers spend a month or two on a detailed outline, then take a month to actually write the book. Some writers start with a title, some write chapters out of order and then put it all together like a puzzle.

And on and on and on.

Every writer is different. Every writer's method is different *There is no correct, mandated way to write a book. Just your way.*

The Myth of Writing Slow to Write Better Actually Hurts Writers

There are two sides of our brains. The creative side and the critical side.

The creative side has been taking in stories since the writer started reading, knowing how to put words together at a deep level. The critical side lags far, far behind the creative side, learning rules that some English teacher or parent forced into the critical mind.

The creative side is always a much better writer than the critical side. Always. It never switches, no matter how long you write.

Long-term (20 years and up) professional writers have learned to trust that creative side and we tend to not mess much with what it creates for us. Of course, this lesson for most of us was learned the hard way, but that's another long chapter for another book.

A new writer who believes the myth that all good fiction must be written slowly and labor-intensive (called work) suddenly one day finds that they have written a thousand words in 35 minutes. The new writer automatically thinks, "Oh, my, that has to be crap. I had better rewrite it."

What has just happened is that the wonderful writing the creative side of the mind has just produced is then killed by the critical side, dumbed down, voice taken out, anything good and interesting removed.

All caused by this myth.

And professional editors in New York are no better, sadly. I once got a rewrite request on a major book from my editor. I agreed with about nine-tenths of the suggestions, so I spent the next day rewriting the book, fixing the problems, and was about to send the manuscript back when Kris stopped me.

The conversation went something like this:

"Don't send it, sit on it a few weeks," Kris said, looking firm and intense, as only Kris can look.

"Why not?" I asked, not remembering at that moment that the myth was a major part of traditional publishing.

"The editor will think you didn't work on it and that it is crap," Kris said.

"But I agreed and fixed everything," I said, starting to catch a clue, but not yet willing to admit defeat.

Kris just gave me that "stare" and I wilted, knowing she was completely correct.

I held the rewrite for three weeks, sent it back with a letter praising the rewrite comments and a slight side comment about how hard I had worked on them, even though I wrote most of another book in the period of time I was holding the rewrite. Story ended happily, editor was happy and commented on how fast I managed to get the rewrites done, all because Kris remembered the myth and how it functions.

Now, let me do something that just annoys people. I'm going to do the math.

The Math of Writing Fast

This chapter when finished is going to be around 2,000 words. That is about 8 manuscript pages with each page averaging 250 words per page.

So say I wrote only 250 words, one manuscript page per day on a new novel.

It takes me about 15 minutes, give-or-take (depending on the book and the day and how I'm feeling) to write 250 words of fiction. (Each writer is different. Time yourself.)

So if I spent that 15 minutes per day writing on a novel, every day for one year, I would finish a 90,000-plus word novel, a large paperback book, in 365 days.

I would be a one-book-per-year writer, pretty standard in science fiction and a few other genres.

15 minutes per day equals one novel per year.

Oh, my, if I worked really, really hard and managed to get 30 minutes of writing in per day, I could finish two novels in a year.

And at that speed I would be considered fast. Not that I typed or wrote fast, just that I spent more time writing.

God forbid I actually write four pages a day, spend an entire hour per day sitting in a chair! I would finish four novels a year. At that point I would be praised in the romance genre and called a hack in other genres.

See why I laugh to myself when some writer tells me they have been working really, really hard on a book and it took them a year to write? What did they do for 23 hours and 45 minutes every day?

The problem is they are lost in the myth. Deep into the myth that writing must be work, that it must be hard, that you must "suffer for your art" and write slowly.

Bull-puckey. Writing is fun, easy, and enjoyable. If you want hard work, go dig a ditch for a water pipe on a golf course in a steady rain on a cold day. That's work. Sitting at a computer and making stuff up just isn't work. It's a dream job.

Spend More Time in the Chair

Oh, oh, I just gave you the secret to being a "fast" writer or a "prolific" writer. Just spend more time writing.

I am the world's worst typist. I use four fingers, up from two, and if I can manage 250 words in fifteen minutes I'm pretty happy. I tend to average around 750-1,000 words per hour of work. Then I take a break. I am not a "fast" typist, but I am considered a "fast" writer because I spend more time writing than the myth allows.

That's the second thing that makes this myth so damaging to writers. It doesn't allow writers to just spend more time practicing their art. In fact, the myth tells writers that if they do spend more time working to get better, they are worse because they produce more fiction.

Writing is the only art where spending less time practicing is considered a good thing.

In music we admire musicians who practice ten or more hours a day. Painters and other forms of artists are the same. Only in writing does the myth of not practicing to get better come roaring in.

We teach new writers to slow down, to not work to get better, to spend fewer and fewer hours at writing, to not practice, and then wonder why so many writers don't make it to a professional level.

We No Longer Have to Wait for Traditional Publishers

For the last few decades, unless a writer wrote under many pen names, we were forced by the market to write fewer books per year. But now, with indie publishing, we can once again write as much as we want.

And we can write anything we want.

We can sell some books to traditional publishers, we can indie publish other books and stories. Or as I am doing, we can create our own market and indie publish almost everything.

The new world has lifted the market restrictions on speed of writing. Now those of us who actually want to sit and write for more than 15 minutes per day can publish what we write in one way or another.

And being fast, meaning spending more time writing, is a huge plus with indie publishing. We are in a new golden age of fiction, especially short fiction, and just as in the first golden age, writing fast (meaning spending more time at your art) will be a good thing also for your pocketbook.

Writing Slow Equals Writing Better is a complete myth, a nasty sacred cow of publishing that hurts and stops writers who believe it.

—The truth is that no two writers work the same and no book is the same as the previous book or the next book.

—The truth is that writing fast is nothing more than spending more time every day writing.

—The truth is that there should be no rule about speed relating to quality.

—The truth is there should be no rule that lumps all writers into one big class. There should only be your way of writing.

Be Careful!

Sadly, this myth is firm in the business, so writers who spend more time in the chair and who write more hours have to learn to work around the myth. We must learn to play the game that teachers, editors, book reviewers, and fans want us to play.

And if you decide you can spend more hours every day writing and working on your art, be prepared to face those who want you to write the way they do. Be prepared to face those who want to control your work. Be prepared to face criticism from failed writers (reviewers) who can't even manage a page a day, let alone more.

This speed myth is the worst myth of an entire book full of myths. Caution.

The best thing you can do is just keep your speed and your writing methods to yourself. Don't write in public as I am doing. You're an artist. Respect your way of doing things and just don't mention them to anyone.

Also, I beg of you that if you believe in the myth, please don't do the math about my age. I sold my first novel when I was 38 and have published over 100 novels. At one book per year, I must be at least 138 years old.

After my hard, single-page-of-writing every day, I sometimes feel that way.

Yeah, right.

But I stand by that story except when I am writing in public on my blog. (grin)

ABOUT THE AUTHOR

USA Today bestselling writer Dean Wesley Smith published more than a hundred novels in thirty years and hundreds of short stories across many genres.

He wrote a couple dozen *Star Trek* novels, the only two original *Men in Black* novels, Spider-Man and X-Men novels, plus novels set in gaming and television worlds. He wrote novels under dozens of pen names in the worlds of comic books and movies, including novelizations of a dozen films, from *The Final Fantasy* to *Steel* to *Rundown*.

He now writes his own original fiction under just the one name, Dean Wesley Smith. In addition to his upcoming novel releases, his monthly magazine called *Smith's Monthly* premiered October 1, 2013, filled entirely with his original novels and stories.

Dean also worked as an editor and publisher, first at Pulphouse Publishing, then for *VB Tech Journal*, then for Pocket Books. He now plays a role as an executive editor for the original anthology series *Fiction River*.

For more information go to www.deanwesleysmith.com, www. smithsmonthly.com or www.fictionriver.com.

The
WMG Writer's Guide
Series

How to Write a Novel in Ten Days

*Think Like a Publisher 2014: A Step-By-Step Guide
to Publishing Your Own Books*

Killing the Top Ten Sacred Cows of Publishing

*Deal Breakers 2013:
Contract Terms Writers Should Avoid*

*The Pursuit of Perfection:
And How It Harms Writers*

*Surviving the Transition: How Writers Can Thrive
in the New World of Publishing*

Printed in Great Britain
by Amazon

38246857R00047